Michael P. McManus

The Buddha Knot

The
Buddha
Knot

Poetry by

Michael P. McManus

Acknowledgments: *The Atlanta Review*, Out There; *West Wind Review*, 1969; *The Adirondack Review*, The Fire Keeper; *Burnside Review*, Sojourn; *Texas Review*, Inmate; *Sulphur River Literary Review*, Elegy for my Grandfather; *The Louisiana Review*, Drought; *Rattle*, Dusk in a Mountain Cemetery; *Poems and Plays*, Reaching for the Dead; *Prism International*, Assuming Spring; *Louisiana Literature*, Opening Day; *The Lyric*, The Long Fisherman; *Midwest Quarterly*, Dead Bird; *Raintown Review*, Wild; *Poetry Southeast*, Autopsy; *Poems and Plays*, Pleasure; *Reed Magazine*, Cold; *Rattle*, Wreckage; *Pebble Lake Review*, Dog; *Louisiana Literature*, Gustav; *Texas Review*, Riding a Horse; *kaleidowhirl*, Slate Run; *Epiphany*, Big Sky; *Louisiana Review*, Plath; *Rhino*, Circle; *Bayou*, Fear; *Rattle*, Notes from the Health Club; *West Wind Review*, The Mud Flats; *Louisiana Literature*, This Morning; *Rattle*, As Fire, my Father; *Louisiana Literature*, The Dying Cowboy; *Louisiana Literature*, Wrestling with God, Buddhism, and Quantum Physics; *Wind Magazine*, The End of Something; *riprap*, Apprentice; *Hawk & Whippoorwill poems of man & nature*, Watcher; *Square Lake*, Hidden Pond; *Penwood Review*, Mount Kenya; *Rattle*, Reunion; *The Meadow*, Corpsman; *Chrysalis Reader*, The Buddha Knot.

The Buddha Knot
©2018 Michael P. McManus
Cover image: Licensed by Prolific Press Inc.
Published by Prolific Press Inc. Johnstown, PA. (USA)
ISBN: 978-1-63275-127-0
Edited by Glenn Lyvers
Assistant editor: April Zipser
Printed in the USA

*For Nana who wanted a poet in the family.
For my Father who told me, "Work hard,
play hard, take time to dream."*

Contents...

Out There

- *For Wayne Magee*

Thirty years after Saigon,
the living room couch holds you
in its cockpit. Above the room
the ceiling fan churns,
each sharp spin a rotor.
Summer heat of the delta
creeps into the house,
flies strafe the screen,
the sun lashes down.
I gather more beer,
nearly slushy from time in the freezer.
You talk about the VA Ward
in Shreveport, the medication
of remembering past comforts:
alcohol and Asian women.
Slowly the day slithers away,
deeper greens turning to black.
Water buffalo flock the streets,
sloshing through rice paddies.
Looking out the window, you tell me,
buddy it's a war out there,
and part your hair with bamboo fingers,
each eye glazed the color of coal.
I say "sleep in the spare room
that's ringed with sandbags and razor wire."
Angry boys fresh from high school
will patrol the perimeter.
At 0200, after an hour's rest,
I am awakened by the muzzle blast
from shattered beer bottles
and a drunken voice crouched
in the street shouting,
incoming.

The Buddha Knot

I turned 22 in the hills of Yokoska, Japan.
A cold spring, winter's separation was indistinct,
blurred, like space between an ant's abdomen and earth.

Mount Fuji, sacred mountain, first panel
of the mind's mirror as written in the ancient text,
stood enormous on the horizon. Snow on its summit

was worshipped as *kami*, divine spirit. Many days,
two hundred miles away, I stared north, dreamed myself
the archer's arrow who shot from the bow, flew

in perfect arc, then plunged down the crater.
That morning, half-sun hidden like a yellow ear behind Fuji,
I walked wet streets, narrow *chaunis*, twisting up steep inclines

like black fingers. After twenty minutes, I reached a small *soudou*,
the meditation hall, where I removed my American aesthetics:
Reeboks, a Steeler's cap. Inside, Shirata Rinjiro was seated in Zazen.

He motioned to join him. One hour later, my legs lost circulation,
ankles ached beneath their torso. Letting go, letting go…
When I extend my hands, he placed into my palms

one length of unremarkable rope. His directions—
This is the Buddha knot, untangle it. Into focus,
a black-metal incense burner. Fuji's tapestry through
    an open window.

I rose, walked across the straw-matted floor, each step filled
   with needles,
my diffusion of self, lost in action, I dropped one end into
   the burner,
watched a flame climb, coil, consume, felt heat on my hand,
   dropped rope

into an empty urn. Minutes later, ashes. I returned to Zazen
   with Rinjiro,
humbly pushed my answer before him. A ten-minute silence,
then a divine laugh, a final direction from beneath his closed eyes.

Good, now untangle it again.

1969

On the day before the viewing,
I went to the mortician without telling my parents,
because they would try to talk me out of it.
After listening to my demands,
he took me to see what I had only seen before
in foreign lands. In the clean and quiet room—
pale, bloodless, embalmed—
the body lay on a stainless-steel table.
Before a boy's powdered face
the color of flour, I stopped believing in angels.
The size of a tomato, a faint bruise
on his temple marked the place
where the truck's grill knocked him from his bike.
I wanted to hold his hands. A few months ago
they found a calling on the playground,
where he spent countless hours
shooting jump shots like Johnny Havlicek.
A white piece of paper the size of a dollar
was tied to his toe. I wanted to know
how it could be possible for anyone to forget
the name of a ten-year-old boy,
as he lay sprawled face down in the rain
on a busy city street, so I folded his name
and placed it in my pocket. Upon kissing his lips,
a certain lunacy made me want to cry in hopes
the echoes my tears made on the tiled floor
would make him laugh again.
But I could not cry because I was twenty-one
and home from Asia where I learned that tears
or gospel songs never bring back the dead.
All things then were real and wrong.
Two days later a platoon of sixteen longhaired Vets
following the hearse on their chopped Harleys,
rode as brothers to take my brother home.

Inmate

I listen for a sound to remind me I am human,
some soft wing beat sweeping the air,
a rattle from the wind's sabers.

But nothing arrives, no feet
from rats steeped in humanity,
nor the crow's anchorite cry.

I miss the wasp sting,
smell of ragweed, watery boils
of poison ivy raking my back.

The walls of my cell are now a skin I wear—
bones of steel and concrete that acquire
my years: a deaf, blind man
who remains my only companion.

Here time is an enigma, a chaste mistress who once loved
with tears. Night and day are dead faces,
blankets of dust lifted by wind,
the tick of the clock as valuable as salt in sand.

In dreams, I see panthers walking the sidewalks,
mountain streams flowing through air,
vagaries of a world ablaze with the thunderous
jumping of horses over ocean waves.

But when I awaken the sun's collapse is imminent,
lost to the day's strangulation.
The flame of the inner I burns to a crescent scar,
a hole in the night where a galaxy should be.

To have loved the stars is a terrible thing.

Poem for Bob

Bob, tonight it's eighteen years since I saw you a final time.
You were wild-eyed, drunk, staggering seaside down the boardwalk

at Mission Beach. I'm sitting here drinking a long neck
and looking out the window at the moon. I'm trying

to makes sense of things. Not this night, but *things.*
Like your unwavering belief that God was a Junkie,

and humans were his fix. It makes sense.
Babies get blown to bits by snipers in Bosnia,

school kids pack firepower in platoons.
In Viet Nam, while defending a dirt hill,

you killed sixty-one Viet Cong.
You were awarded a silver star;

for heroic actions in overwhelming fields of enemy fire.
Years later, after smoking a joint,

the Navy proclaimed the former marine, *unfit for duty.*
Christ, Bob, in a few months I turn thirty-nine.

Your age when we sat together in dark bars examining life
in our reflections on beer bottles. I still drink too much.

My damaged leg has gotten worse. And I write poetry.
Yes, Poetry. If you read this, I'm sure you would shake your head,

finger your red Irish hair, and ask if I betrayed our moments?
Poetry will always seem sappy to some people. I don't care.

No writer who believes in this craft writes for them.
I write for people like you.

People brave enough to share their souls
and never ever ask for a receipt. Like that night

in San Diego when we slammed Tequila shots.
On the jukebox, someone played Led Zepplin over and over.

You talked openly with me about life in-country.
The return home. Nightmares like rubber balls inside your head.

Sometimes this scar over my left eye makes me laugh
if I remember your backwards headbutt from that night

just because I locked you in a bear hug to keep you from a fight.
It became a poem. Not the headbutt, but the rest:

Those words, moments, emotions, and theories fell to paper.
A small college journal has agreed to publish your night.

One day, I hope the poem finds you because the truth is there
in the light that only you would understand. It belongs to you

and no one else. Bob, before I leave, I miss you, Brother.
Wherever you walk, I pray our god has proven you wrong.

The Fire Keeper
- For E.L. Moran

Though a wing could carry more weight than your arms,
I watched you walk out back beside the barn,

where traces of windblown snow-covered logs
you cut and piled last year with wrists

twice as thick as the ax-handle in your hands,
those spent husks, frail as the moment

when a falling star is suddenly visible, then lost.
You bent over and placed your hands on the cold bark,

each vein in your arms as thin as a longitude line.
I sensed that you believed the place where you stood

was nearly imagined like a constellation's stick-figures.
Quick breath plumes, smoky though silent, drifted

above your head, a magician's frosty helmet,
which was less tremulous, but as revealing

as the cancer's sleight-of-hand. For years,
it performed its black magic for an audience of one.

From where I stood on the back porch,
I heard you first curse, then laugh, a comet

granted rest from its orbit.
You stood upright with three pieces of split-oak in your arms,

cradling them as if they were charmed,
then turned to slowly face me like an oncoming eclipse.

Never had the way to build a fire been so beautiful.
And the sky, vaporous, blue, deep, carried on without you.

Sojourn
- For J.I.

Think praxis, that place where sky dissolves
into space, or an open space,
                              or how it will not matter
when the spark-lit tinder ignites under your hands.

Think asymmetry, the body's warmth
& the Spanish Moss aflame;
                              one red scarf twisting
skyward, a nexus for the child crying in a velvet field,
bruised at last by the swinging gates of God.

You are not the man within that passing.
You are my father without the chest tubes,
                              laughing in a bright room

years before it turned dark as the pulsing metastasis
spiking your stomach.
                    What Buddha nature
can now define your gasping?

From no-one's making, everything was made finite.
For six straight months, we spent weekends hiking the gorge,

exploring washouts, noting shale formations,
                              and wading ankle-deep
into the bronze-colored river.

Little did we know our days had begun to dissolve
like limestone pumped full of water.
                              Some days, Lord,
should remain to be spilled back upon us
        without a ripple.

But not this day of sunlight that dazzles canyon walls,
                                   & brightens thousands of black birds
darting in single formation above the water.

I turn to watch them fly into the future,
with a rush of wings
                         that tell us goodbye.

The Double Son

Dressed in robes and rituals by the clinical acolytes,
they await their gods in separate temples.

Like the fervor of prayers in the Holy Land,
radiation begins to fry their bodies like bacon grease.

All that's missing, *Adagio for Strings*.
Later they receive the chemo drip,

their veins bruised by the all-too-familiar needle pricks
releasing one million starved wolverines

that run wild in a feeding frenzy on white blood cells.
In Pennsylvania, it's a season for cancer:

not the constellation clutching its starry pattern,
but a terrible missive many are forced to read.

The final paragraph refuses to change its ending,
nor its exclamation point toppled and trampled by our language,

which we foolishly believe speaks the myth
to someone else's killer who begins its life

as an unknown pandemic castaway.
It's little more than a pencil mark X'ed on a leaf.

Falling from its tree in the predawn hours,
who or what hears the writhing birth of its syllables

before they reach the physician's tongue?
Esophageal/Prostate. Father/Stepfather.

My life stands before their blinding brightness.
Now they are marooned on concrete islands.

A blanketing fog hides the comforts they wish for
in the Alleghenies, where each day is spent waiting

for me to swim the rising current,
navigate the flotsam of double doors.

They swing open to reveal other forced smiles.
All along the polished waiting room's beaches,

plastic palm trees grow beside flat screen tv's
projecting a cyanic paradise.

They want us to see
nymphs frolicking in waterfalls.

not the litter just off the beaten path,
stench of vomit, fallen clumps of hair.

All this must be equal to the beast that will come.
I stop and close my eyes.

Some days to find the music,
you must first listen to the silence.

We have lived so long without it,
flying forward towards these moments

like wind through an ocean of grass.
As it sways, it sways together.

Suddenly blackbirds wheel from trees,
gathering air under their wings.

Some will surely die.
I watch until they go.

Two men, beloved, as only Fathers can be.
I love them wholly and remain buoyed by it.

Then the attractive middle-aged nurse,
recently divorced (she told me that)

and with admiration for men who write poetry,
enters the room. Her touch is hallelujah

as it rests upon my shoulder.
Her blue eyes narrow. The muse looks out.

Knowing this afternoon will see me drive
one-hundred miles from this, my stepfather's hospital,

to my father's hospital, to repeat the unimaginable,
I wonder if I should give thanks or be ashamed.

On days like this when it is easy to remain a child,
she has the audacity to show me how I am still a man.

I-20

At night, I walk out to the interstate.
Bright lights pass before me like meteor showers.
So many of them flying by,
they could be like souls, if you think like that.
And I do. A long time
I stand in the roadside margin,
where no one sees me,
shadowed by Louisiana pines.
Perhaps this is how
some of us come to meet our God.
We gaze into the stars,
no matter where we find them.

Trying to Remember that First Kiss

Much like the beekeeper's philosophy
of entering a kind of loneliness
with something that will sting
once he removes his protective suit
around the buzzing hives,
      it is a perfect mistake
to go back, to reconstruct the enigma
from those moments following what was the *moment.*
Call it a common wind passing
through the lattice into the other side,
which is nothing more than the side before it,
a season growing cold or warm.
       Often, I remember
that sweet warm change the week winter turned
to premature spring in Pennsylvania.
Creeks ran high with snowmelt melody.
From the bright skies, it seemed Heaven had cracked
wide open and floated down
this radiance.
    We were
sixteen—our bodies hiding places
for the awkward blindness, we wanted to feel
our way through.
     We found a dry place
with a wrinkled bed of grass under the spruce.
And I still remember the luxury of lying there, helpless,
ready to be bruised by what was not yet understood.
And then her kiss lingered in the air like incense,
her body the censer from which it drifted

to now, which means nothing. I mean no ellipsis,
no comma, nothing but the tiny black
period, a primal end stop.
                              Such memories are
beautiful, useless ghosts
                              like those bedroom walls
from my childhood home. They have been replaced by a factory
filled with gears, levers, and ratchets. Those hard edges show divisions
of labor, the absence of curves. And flesh?
It produces nothing but artifice. Each morning
the paperboy pedals down the cracked sidewalk,
and tosses unto my front porch.
I walk outside, come back in, and sit down
to read what I will likely not remember.

Elegy for my Grandfather

A beach of snow, and beyond it, almost too far to see,
    a single gull hovers
above glinting waves. They curl and crest,
    exalt their brief permanence
before a final crash and backrush towards the sea,

which, at best, brings one more accretion,
    the downdrift
swirl of sand along the headland,
or over time, upland scarps rising from the backshore.

This day, a salty wind blows pellets of ice
    inland
glittering the dunes with an almost painful whiteness.

Still, the evening sky shows gold as any crown we give
    to kings,
a stark contrast to all things hidden beneath
the dark-green swells the gull
    now climbs steeply over

on wings diminished by flight until, at last,
it lines up with the sun,
and there suffices the moment,
which in its sudden becoming,

defines a silhouette ringed by brightness,
    an aura
glowing beyond any recognition
I can give this place except for these memories:

this beach, its salt marshes in spring,
    a boy
wandering the berms with his grandfather,
asking endless questions

about breakwaters, riprap and estuaries,
neap tides and storm surges,
the slow erosion of all we cannot keep.

Drought

Back in port with ten days of leave,
I reread Ellen's letter, the woman I left for the Navy.
I threw a rucksack into my jeep and left the bustle of Norfolk.
Drove past a million bleary truck stops,
through the endless green hills of Pennsylvania.
Northeast of nowhere and with eight hours lost
beneath my tires, I began to climb Stony Gap Road.
The gravel curves along this switchback remained unchanged.
So did those ramshackle houses. Engine blocks sat rusting
beside tractor tires with roses planted inside.
Even time grew tired.
                              Near the summit
the etched wooden placard read *Zen and the Burning Bush,*
a road as dry as sawdust leading to a single-story
frame house, tin roof, fresh coat of yellow paint,
stained-glass windows shining in the sun.
Bone-thin, barefoot, wearing chino shorts.
A wide-brimmed felt hat covering the head
bleached bald by chemo. A muscle shirt
no longer stretched tight across your breasts.
Out you came waving as if nothing had changed
in your life. Eagerly and endlessly grinning,
showing off your commissioned paintings,
sculptures, favorable *New York Times* reviews.
I carried a cooler of beer onto the porch.
We shared a joint.
                              You told me,
thirty-seven days without rain.
The lone oak moaned and cracked in the wind.
Fissures snaked back and forth across the ground,
showing where green had turned to brown.
That night under a quarter moon and high stars,
your body light as a second skin against mine,
we made love on a pallet.

Then a sudden coolness came
up the mountain, bringing with it the pines swaying.
As if a debt had been paid, it began to rain.
Steady, strong, like a runner's heartbeat.
Black pools formed in tire ruts.
Runnels poured off the roof.
In the most beautiful dance I have ever witnessed,
you left the porch, laughed in the yard,
curled your toes into the earth.
Three weeks from becoming a ghost,
you exclaimed, *I believe that I can beat this thing…*

Dusk in a Mountain Cemetery

The grass stands as high as the season
allows it to grow. The retired white church, time-tumbled,

decrepit, accepts its own defeat. Generous arms
from the oaks give it shade, swallows nest in broken gables.

Who would abandon such a place? A tombstone:
Beloved daughter of James and Mary Conner, born 1814, died

1822, R.I.P., is near erosion's end. Soon this flat stone
will be no more than what the ground can tell us.

In a lower field, a black horse waits for a young boy
who runs and waves. The horse flags its tail,

lowers its head, as the boy, impossible to define from this distance,
grabs its mane, fluently pulls himself onto the bare back.

Up through the stillness come horse and rider, out of something
I cannot touch, a sense of history that held its breath and expired.

They pass down the dirt road in front of the church,
unaware of my presence. Perhaps this is best.

What would a child think if he found a strange man standing
at dusk among the ruins of a mountain cemetery?

Seven hills away I watch as the sun begins to shut its eye,
and I see the image of myself as this coming darkness.

Reaching for the Dead

Across lean fields I walk in winter,
the far river frozen, a white stain on water.

This morning I opened your final letter,
a stone through a window, words spilling
like glass on my feet.

Now snow deepens; for all its brightness
it blinds.

My fingers curl like burning paper,
yet give no heat: the language
of your touch is forever lost.

Reaching the river, I kneel,
place my hands down
to imprint the ice, numb skin.

Rising, I touch my face,
imagine yours:
bright flesh turned to shadow.

It is like holding ash from a star.

The sun breaks from the sky,
in its inadequate warmth
I recall your moments, still on my skin.

It's midnight in the bedroom,
where a single light burns into the unreachable distance.

On the back porch, there is a sudden
rush of wind, and I hear the creak
of our empty swing.

Opening Day

It returns with the most unexpected signs.
Like the car or truck that just slammed on its brakes
to send me back in time until I am walking
along a snowy stream in November
late enough in the day so that each bare
tree is moving into its own darkness.

So many events that I cannot remember
have moved on to other places in the long,
hard hours of my life, but still I remember
a single sparrow perched on a branch
and fluffed against the cold. It seemed artificial;
when I walked near enough to touch
a wing nothing moved but the wind.
The half-frozen waters of the stream
captured whatever light it could from the sun.
In parts of the deep cut bank the water disappeared
into something dark and den-like.

If the world were mine for a minute,
that day when I was sixteen
would not have happened and the sparrow
would have long ago flown fast away to summer.
But the God of my days sends across the years
a gunshot so close I still hear it ringing,
followed by the balanced silence
of something real and wild gone quiet.

The white-tail went thrashing through brambles
down a wooded hill, but when I raised my rifle
and focused the scope for a second shot,
found only hunter's orange. Terror, terror,
and more terror covered the man's face
as he ran weaving toward a piney thicket.

Near a fence post I found the body,
though he still lived as blood bubbled
from his mouth like a child playing vampires..

The snowy ground was a freshly painted red
and went steaming up around him like the soul
that was leaving. Trembling as all things must
tremble as the moth called life approaches
its final fire, the gut-shot man reached
out his arm to touch his foolish hunter,
and then stepped back in fear.
Crouched against a tree he began to shiver
as in a winter nightmare where he's lying naked
in bed without a blanket to cover his body,
powerless to move as the windows break.

Assuming Spring

Assuming it was Spring, you called from a foreign port
to tell me the new job was fine, then asked about deer feeding

in the old orchard, if fields were plowed and seeded?
I stood by the closed window where a red maple's shadow

swayed into the den like an unsettled dream. Your voice,
impenetrable as lush undergrowth, continued to sprout

with questions, ten-thousand hammer taps on a tin can,
all the same imperatives impaled on ritual. I went outside

and walked you through the morning air, over the hard
grass, burred nettles, fresh coyote tracks,

hay and field rock stacked behind the barn.
There the white hidden ground stretched for miles.

Closing in on every side, the sky grayed
its myopic heart. I told you the weather was exceptional,

marjoram and goldenrod flourished, our horses pounded
across bright meadows. When I reached the pond,

I described the measured sounds of fleeing ducks,
as I walked shore to shore across solid ice.

The Lone Fisherman

No one sees him walk the dry gravel bed
along the silent creek. His feet curl over rocks,
stiffen for balance, branches crown his head,
trawl his heavy shoulders like a green smock.

Sometimes he moves as if wounded and bruised,
drifts away like a cloud on the horizon.
His steps are words, a language that grew
from the sound of water moist against his skin.

Six hours and nothing but dust, an old tire
sunk in the channel, the glint of broken glass.
A dead bike, still searching for its rider,
attempts to hook him with its rusting grasp.

He stops, unloops his line as if lost in dream,
and with a dancer's grace, casts to a phantom stream.

The Feeding

The eighty-eight-year-old widow
who lives next door is outside again.
For twelve straight days in January
the temperature has not risen
above freezing. And yet, each morning
her parka-clad, hunched body has appeared
in her front yard. Today, as before,
she moves like a human divining rod,
searching among maples and oaks,
her skin nearly hidden beneath God
knows how many layers
of clothes, her eyes like a baby's
looking up at her mother.
She chooses a place and stops,
begins to sway back and forth,
back and forth; a pendulum rocking
as the sky turns black and descends
upon her one kiss at a time:
crow, sparrow, wren,
each drawn by fragile hands
that scatters birdseed across the lawn.
The birds have acquired an instinct
that something given so freely
will not last forever without trust.
And so they sing and that is enough.

Dead Bird

Not much left now but skull and beak,
A few feathers on hollow bones,
And the tiny, crab-like feet
That clung to wires and limbs.

Does the song leave us when we die?
Will the soul suffer for the body's guise?
I could stop here and begin to dance
Along the curb, throw up my arms

Under the great winter maples,
Like a wild man embracing his madness.
If I did, my neighbors would gather on porches,
Or look out windows, asking what was wrong with me.

Though the sweetness it brings to me
May sound to others like grief,
How could I make them believe I have chosen
To have faith in the dead bird's song?

Autopsy

Lay my naked body belly-up on a stainless-steel table.
Place my watch and wedding ring inside a rubber box.
Now raise my head unto a wooden block.
Take the surgeon's Stryker saw;
Make a scalp incision ear to ear. Be careful
not to cut your fingers. Take hammer and chisel,
tap, tap, tap around the skull, pull my cap.
Gently remove my brain, examine it for lesions,
bruises, thoughts of you. Somewhere
is a snowy Vermont with hemlock woods,
our mountain honeymoon, laughter on skis.
Log your findings, move on to my eyes,
closely examine them in their sockets,
take them out. They offer no reflection,
yet still they stare only at you.
Open my mouth, look at my tongue.
Can you remember its truths, its lies?
The many, many times it wet your skin?

Pick up a clean scalpel, begin with an incision
on the left shoulder, descend, pass under
the nipples, ascend to the right shoulder.
Pull the cutanous piece upward and back,
make a medium incision from the margin
of the previous cut down to the pubic region.
Cut through muscle, expose my ribs,
ignore my body's shaking as you separate bone,
and plunge your hands into my thoracic cavity
where you take hold of my heart. Press your fingertips
on its four chambers, each a house of love
and anger, remorse, inexhaustible desire
until now when all the livid blood is stilled.
Record some notes, move quietly down
the abdomen, touch the flaccid penis,

the shriveled testicles. Recall our daring
energies when we were young,
slow murmurs of pleasure, our children.
Now wipe your forehead and ask yourself,
is such dissection still the man you love?
If so, piece me together, stitch me tight,
take me home, or put this thing to rest.

Wild

At first, he grunts before he flails about
the Jeep in ways no man should see his son.
The seatbelt strains as he begins to shout
and tilt his head to stare into the sun.
We leave the road and bounce across a field
still wet from storms that always make him scream.
I watch his face. He does not try to shield
it when the tires spin in mud. What dream
is deep enough to keep him locked away,
or touch the world as if it's broken glass?
But then, be still, it seems he wants to say—
six whitetail deer are watching from the grass.
I let him out to walk across the land.
Perhaps to the only things he understands.

Pleasure

One inch from your temple, I hold a handgun,
a growling dog held at bay by a worn leash.

On your hands and knees, held
to earth by a single finger,
your eyes are a wide canyon;

no bridge exists to span its mountains
of disbelief.

In all things lurks an ending.
Nights when momma slept like a shadow,
you crept into my bedroom,
door hinges oiled with silence.

I sank with no way to surface,
listened to your approach,
whiskey hanging on your breath,
a lion's necklace.

My cries were never heard from the forest.
Imprisoned, I bled beneath
those hands, sharkskin.

For twenty years I have awakened
nights, recalled your chilling words,
'the pleasure is all mine.'

Now your world rests inside
a spinning chamber, you look
to plea bargain, extend a shaking arm.

I set the dog free to bite.
The pleasure is mine.

Cold

All our marriage I've come to expect these things from you.
Yes, I wear Gore-Tex if my beard begins to freeze,
or when a crystal Rorschach spiders the window,
through which I've looked outside and seen
a sugar-white field with deer feeding in threes.

A little dialogue goes a long way when pipes burst.
We know that no flooding will come
until what's broken thaws again.
And so, you belly up the best you can
to show me what's vulnerable in a man.

Your magnitude fills the ponds with ice
as gravity sleets from the sky, while other nights
the forest retreats into the silence of monkhood.
But just once I wonder if you could forego your verity—
take a chance and sear the cherry trees

on Orchard Hill into blossom, show me one place
where a heart-red summer solstice will melt the snow.

War-Torn

The blood of the brave spills from the tremors in your mouth.
Cold winds of war blow through wounded eyes.
When you walk, each step touches down
in another freshly laid minefield.

Your hair smells like a six-month hump in the jungle.
It's tangled with mosquitoes and tropical rains.
Your face stays covered with camo grease
that reinforces your thousand-yard stare.

Nights when the moon flares like a mortar,
you crawl across the ground, a heavy shadow,
always waiting for the sharp pierce
of searing shrapnel to puncture your heart.

Come morning your battleground is littered
with the amputated limbs of yesterday's sorrows,
and a single white cross marking the spot,
where our love lies buried, a posthumous hero.

Wreckage

Maria, should you hear these words, then by some final
fate, my prayers are answered. Moments ago, the jet
shuddered, now smoke is in the forward seats.

How high we are I do not know, nor does it matter,
Maria, for those who share this place are hostages
with little chance to escape. I can see the left engine

spitting oil. The captain's voice sounds somber and shaken.
Now the jet has begun to tilt and dive. Maria,
people are screaming, yet I feel some strange calm

in this seat. Outside, clouds pass like white sheets,
and two seats forward, an infant stares at me
with wondrous eyes as I talk into this hand recorder.

Beside me, a Rabbi cries for his wife. For once
in my life, I wish something worthy of these fingers,
and so I reach over and touch his tears.

I wonder now about sin and the soul, if the thousand
lies I told you wait now to greet me. We have broken
the clouds. The sun fills the fuselage and illuminates

the terror. Where is faith, the ache for the other side?
Oxygen masks hang from their tethers. Some passengers
wear them, others embrace and pray, and some

bend forward, face down on their final pillows.
Maria, I feel a soft rapture that's difficult to explain,
and words, however explicit or mundane, fail me.

I see the earth now, its small ribbons of streams,
squared green fields, brown thickets. I have never
felt such joy, here winged, plunging beyond time,

the great face of God rising…

Dog

Like the last living thing left from the Donner Party,
the coal-black dog would slink to our back porch
after crossing the gravel mountain road—
a dusty helix that spiraled through woods as green and alive
as any childhood dream I remember.

I remember rationing my meals,
hoarding chicken wings, bones,
bits of bread and half-eaten hamburgers
I cached under my bed
until the time was right.

The time was mostly right in the early morning
or at dusk when my father was away,
preoccupied in fields that I would come to hate
because among the greening husks of corn
I had no life to choose but my father's.

But I could choose my life when my father stayed away.
Fearful at first, the dog would snarl and snap,
then whimper as it bellied along the earth
until it reached my feet and stopped
to eat gently from my hands.

I am thankful that I can remember my hands
when they were young and eager for the world
beyond our gravel road, eager for what was waiting
and what would come loping out of the shadows.
What still might come if I stepped outside and whistled.

Eyepiece

Last night my neighbor's cat caught on fire,
and like a tiny comet flew down the street
before disappearing.

But it was just a dream, because this morning
when I got out of bed to look out my window,
there was Groucho crouched beneath the pin oak.

On a branch above, a squirrel jerked its tail.
After I had dressed, I walked outside
Where the central air's syncopated hum

competed against the cicada's thrum,
the blue jay's intangible cry,
and the sound of a house being built.

If I could, I would blister my hands with work
by hammering nails all day long,
or lugging trusses to frame the roof.

I could dig a ditch and lay the plumbing proper.
But the only tool I own is a pen.
It's more a telescope than anything else.

And lately when I look through the eyepiece,
I see the distant world I want to believe in
as just one more day of make-believe.

Rescue Efforts

- Remembering 9/11

The following day, she comes in carrying a plastic bucket
filled with my leather work gloves,

safety glasses and her plastic shovel.
Petite, bold, wearing a Steelers ballcap,

her tiny strength believes it can
make a difference. Many times,

I scolded her for watching too much TV.
Now she knows New York

as if it's our living room.
But she's still too young to comprehend

the evil. Let her grow up before she begins
to moralize this eternal September.

She goes to put everything back in her closet.
For now, we can leave history behind.

We get into the MDX and drive
to Baskin-Robbins for vanilla ice cream.

Gustav

I see it now, one day out, maybe two,
barrel-chested, roiling forward, the flying fish really *flying*

with the storm-tossed albatross. Here,
two-hundred miles north, we're safe enough

before the prediction of big, big winds,
and heavy rains pouring forth from God's emptiness.

There won't be any lashing down of things.
The wisteria and magnolia seem unaware.

Strapped inside tiny earphones, my Zune charged,
I'm a nearly naked backyard hipster,

a supine dynamo who can almost see
forty's final digit. Relatively speaking,

I'm healthy and tan. Hemingway would be proud
to call me a crony, I think. These minor accomplishments

must speak, dream-like, to me
and my German Shepherd too,

that big-boned black and tan marathoner,
who fetches the thrown tennis ball, forever.

Overhead, a soupy mix of clouds:
grayed, indistinct, any edges blurred,

or perhaps a single cirrus, a face
at the moment of eclipse, longer than the horizon,

the sun its only eye, dulled through prodigal.
Melodies, strong, true, race through thin wires-

Talking Heads – *Psycho Killer* – my foot taps,
Qu'est-ce que c'est?fa fa fa fa fa fa fa fa far better

run run run run run run run away...
Is this the contraflow for artistic license?

Should a poem suffer before the wind?
Everybody must give something back for something they get;

Dylan sings on day two from *The Bootleg Series,*
as the selfless trees sway, perhaps before the same gusts

that swept through Houma and Morgan City.
No tropical storm winds yet, though Max's canine barometer

seems to sense some coming change in this low-key atmosphere.
He keeps pointing his snout into the air turned choir.

Is he trying to capture its song as scent? Perhaps
this is how he sees the Doppler pink and reds,

knowing more than just a front is moving in,
a morning in which he's meant to be a prophet.

Is it the soul, then, a Sergeant-at-arms,
this Dear John to the body human that's suddenly keen

to those minute, self-effacing moments of transcendence
that transcend little or nothing, yet seem Heaven-sent.

Still, whoever I am at this moment is in abundance
beneath this swirling disconnect of darkened sky

that seems, almost, like a siren through the quiet.
And then? Already the leaves are tossed about,

their green sails fluttering as they pull the great ship forward.
And to where? Well, here's as good a harbor as any,

a refuge for rain, which falls now from its own fullness.
Rain is intimate. The drops shine like a constellation.

The wind rises. Power lines twang like guitar strings.
They sing to the sky which no longer feeds on fire.

I laugh as the Milky Way slides down my face.
Orion tightens his belt on my chest.

Everything is empty space begotten by empty space.
In spite of this to which I believe I am privy,

fear has driven me inside to safety.
It is the appearance of some new world order,

if just for a day or two. I want to rock-and-roll
to what remains, to what was always *here;*

an epic in the making. In the end, what holds sway
over me is this: I hope the power doesn't go out.

Riding a Horse

Each year when winter set in,
that special season you loved like a daughter,
you filled your pockets with peeled apples
and climbed the pasture fence,

where at sunset you walked the open meadow
over tender clover covered with snow
to the north stable, a pilgrim's rest
where you softly clicked your tongue

to the white mare named Shadow,
who for love of your crepuscular timbre
night after night galloped with you
through driving snow and silent fields.

On wings made from the star's milky light,
you sought the sky and flung yourselves
to far away ridges where you dreamed
of the wind-swept sound of wild horses.

But when that final spring arrived on crutches,
why did you gently caress her trusting mane,
and dare to trust the ice on a melting river?
Mother, you always were such a poor swimmer.

Years later when tending the new orchard,
I heard a neighbor call out at dark
that you both were a white fire in winter,
who for the simple joy of flight became

the spark's sudden bursting into flame.

Slate Run

One morning far removed
from this time, I walked a lower meadow
where old voices called
from a childhood diminished

to memories of Pennsylvania forests,
cold mountain streams.

The wind lay silent like an empty nest.
Pastures where cattle grazed
in green weather rested beneath a fresh sea of snow.

It covered rolling hills as if a white tent
had fallen from its poles. A distant
strand of oak woods staked
their claim to the land.

I watched stark limbs with few remaining leaves
wait for wind to begin again,
perhaps to sing a secular song,
and I was certain any song I heard
would be a brown and barren ballad.

I walked miles
until I reached a stone wall
built by ancient farmers
who were now forgotten words.

Crows were black bruises in the sky.
Hearing them I was thankful no person
could call my name.

There remain things a man
should listen for before he gives away his eyes
or scatters his remains.

With my back turned away,
I listened to Slate Run
ripple its unmeasured flow.

For long moments, I thought of God
and all his music,
the deafening silence solitude brings,
and wondered if men who had gone before me

were now trees and wind with souls
who watched my body
rise up from a stone wall and startle a wild
white grouse into flight,

the whir of its wings caught forever
in my own time of small fires.
I followed a footpath bordered by bright
cairns of childhood and bird-empty trees.

Light contained the frozen absence of summer,
its poems now encased in ice. Morning sun
like a white blossom lifted over cold ridges
on its porcelain wings.

When I reached the old stream that flashed
over stones, a sounding of echoes
burst forth like grains of light
made whole from a child's eyes.

Peace grew up from the earth.
I cannot explain how I felt my father's touch
as I learned to fish for trout, or heard
my dog funnel through leaves as it chased teasing sparrows.

No, I cannot explain
how it all suddenly emerged,
like a single flower,
grown up from a stony ruin.

Song of Long Po

My love, my love,
I write these words
without paper or pen,
a man-shadow floating in a black river,
silent as the moon scratching the sky.

In the courtyard called the Emperor's Golden Horse,
walls so high they silence Beijing,
Ch'i Ti and I walk daily,
our heads bowed as if asking forgiveness.

But in our feigned sorrows I recite words
that pass like light through a window,
will shine on you when Ch'i Ti is released.

I remember the last time I held you in Tiananmen Square.
Tanks like elephants,
their steel skin tattooed with red stars,
lumbered down the street.

We watched Lao Tzu kneel in peace.
Brave as a tiger, fragile as a lotus blossom,
but crushed like a flea under those tanks as he shouted,
the existence of truth holds more power than any army!

A man learns how to die by living for his beliefs.

When three police officers felled me, six arms moving
as one hatred, I prayed to the Gate of Heavenly Peace.
You stood before me, hands the color of milk
covered your face, your voice a white dove
singing *Long Po, Long Po!*

Each finger of my hands tells a year inside this cell,
they are so filled with time I cannot grasp anything.

You wrote in the only letter I was allowed to receive,
I would give up eternity just to touch you.

I beg of you now give nothing away,
but in your heart touch me for eternity.
The winters are cold, yet I continue to love you
with the passion of a thousand burning flames.
I have little fire left to give
but this song of love,
it is all that will remain
long after my embers have turned to ash.

Meditation at Hoaglands Run

Along its banks the cold, reptilian stream
is lined with snow where flowers used to grow.
A little further out in deeper runs,
the streaming amber sparks where whitecaps leap
above the stony fix of sunken rocks,
flash by so fast like all my summers past.
The sense of self from years ago is gone.
The shrunken child will rise no more at dawn
to chase the day away through fallen leaves.
The eyes that keep a man awake at night
are furthest from the light when morning comes.
Still, here I see the shape of limbs in trees,
the tapered way the highest branches bend
when death is reaching for but fails to catch
a rising riot of red-winged blackbirds.
How can they fly so close yet never touch?
Against the sky they form a single wing;
it flies from what is truest in the earth,
where life demands that men must live as thieves,
that they must steal each moment for themselves,
a place where hope is hell inside a breeze
that blows away the promises they made.
What changes touch the monuments we make,
the fables bought and sold from door to door,
the whores who claim there was a virgin birth?
A proper edifice is proper ice.
It's winter now, a cold becoming calm
is how I see my property from here:
the generational home, neglected but warm,
twin silos that will no longer store
the green, pressed corn through this empty harvest.
The bloated, broken sacrificial lamb
believes it's free until it looks at me
in some blighted holy Hallelujah

as I prepare it for the supper table.
Do I resemble any kind of man
who stays oblivious to the grave that waits,
whether we love or hate, or soon slaughter
the sow and leave its blood along the roadside
margins where people pass in light-filled cars?
There they go, the discarded selves, saplings
as pliant as a single fist of souls
on a boxer who keeps punching at the night,
until we see the stars come sprinkling down.
I want to hear the syncopated thrum
they make and feel the morning after rush.
It is not over yet. I want to watch.
I'll place myself inside the burning chair
to feel the flames that dance around my feet,
and climb the equal legs of wood and flesh.

Unexpected

Its face turns into the ashen face of a sick child.
That might explain its sluggish ways,
or misguided intentions lingering all along
the horizon. But its color is a coming force,

like the brush strokes of Monet, or an ocean revealed
for the first time. Then the wind increases.
Birds hide in leafy pockets. People stay inside.
But I go out back to stand under the downcast sky.

It's as if an old man has exercised
his life's devotion and decided it's time to die.
We are immeasurable in such moments,
a subtle crease along the edge of dark and light.

The wind quickens like a ghost ship
and the first pellets rain down in darts,
which give way to the machine gun
hidden somewhere in the clouds. I retreat

to the patio and stand beside the helpless grill.
My dog yelps as the backyard explodes to white,
and refuses to come out from his concrete home.
Passing cars become secondary sounds,

and after the dark asphalt is buried in ice,
four- wheel-drives creep sparingly towards town.
One hour later the house lights suddenly flare
to an ethereal brightness. Moments later

all the power in our neighborhood goes out.
Impressive lights crackle on the horizon.
Neon blues and pink shower those places
where transformers burst incandescent inks

into the night. Three rows of red maples,
a multitude of pines, a single magnolia in the minimal
pond of an open thicket, where ripples of ice
cover each branch and leaf, adjoin trunks

to ground in a frozen waterfall,
docile yet defeated, immobile, asking a reprieve?
It arrives at midnight. A strange bird
sings from its glacial nest,

its tiny rickus chipping ice,
alive in the order of things,
flickering beneath the moon's elation.
Glistening pulps, the boughs are lucid pearls

crushed inside a thin glaze,
frozen minnows swim inside them
in the form of bark as glassy tendrils reflect the stars.
Transparent or transfixed,

what has emptied from above
is not forgotten,
but livid like the muzzle of a gun,
from which the rapid sounds

of thick branches breaking free
from time control the history
of where I stand
and where I hope to be.

Big Sky

Three straight nights through these woods
without a flashlight, following the path
I learned in sunlight, guided by jays
and sparrows, ubiquitous pines, the flashing whitetail.

Now the kudzu twists shadows into shadows,
palmetto waits with its stiletto leaves.
Something growls from brambles,
splashes away through brackish water
some call bayou, creek, or slough.

Moon glow allows me to see
places ahead: curves, dips, the last rise
through hanging limbs. Soon I'm sweating,
walking through last year's turnrow,

then, carefully, the summer-dry furrows.
The cicada's ceaseless drone brings Kashmir by Zepplin.
I stop middle field, swat some mosquitoes,
wonder why I'm dreaming back Jimmy Page's fingers
pulling licks faster than a hummingbird's wingbeat.

One more night I've found my big sky
with its three wire thin vapor trails, a half moon,
and those billion tons of glowing gases.
But pure blackness I've come to see,

things I can and cannot comprehend from where I stand.
As I make time tapping my fingers on my thigh,
a little groove work its way through my body,
a little harmony between me, the emptiness,

and the old blues singer down on Bourbon Street,
who told me, *don't worry, boy, the guitar never lies.*

Black Night, Likely Stars

Out here, the screech owl could be love's answer
to despair as it perches on its limb
and screeches the only ode

it knows. Tell me who listens
to this? Yesterday, I killed a field mouse
by striking it on the head

with a sharp blow from my shovel.
And I swear the tiny soul on its release
streamed before my eyes

like gifts of light that were free
at last from its earth-bound piñata.

I threw away that shovel and danced
near the compost pile for John the Apostle,
a long overdue tribute because

he would never dance in Jerusalem,
nor drink with Solomon the pottery maker,

who believed in Jesus,
but felt no sin trading his earthenware
for wine-filled flasks made from goatskin.

Three years of seminary school
taught me this until the Jesuits kicked me out
when I argued that any man

has every right to engage in sodomy
with the woman he loves.

Black night, likely stars.

I love you more when the dead are near me
and moonlight turns the meadow blue
as a New Orleans dirge by Coltrane.

Moon, stay where you are,
I love it that you have no friends
yet continue to shine above our perditions.

Elegy, stop this burning of leaf and limb;
we have no way of knowing
if the textbook illustrations are true,

if all the praise the dead
like ferns in a forest
that rustle around our feet.

Domesticate the bobcat,
pull down the sun in a fit of genius,
or try and find Godot
explaining Medusa away.

Black night, likely stars,

solo embrace of the moon's ligature
tight around my neck,
let me run through everything

and through nothing-
at this hour, all the unchecked bags
are waiting at lost and found.

Black night, likely stars.

Maybe you will last, maybe
you will give me one more chance to ask;

field mouse will you forgive me?

Plath

What is love but a pillar of salt
left in the rain, or dried
paper; hence,
I tend to myself with a nebula of fumes.

Tumescent eyes
that flicker in my face,
I burn past what is beautiful,

and truth or beauty,
be what it may,
throws itself out

the open window.
Down, down, down,
I spiral in magnificent

ways like a ceramic peacock,
or is it I rise inconsequential
on tumultuous waves
and toss about
rose and driftwood?

I pace with the clowns,
dance to the music in churches
or image back time to when I was ten,
Oh, daddy, daddy, how do I look
in pigtails and braces?

This furious scholar who shares
my bed demands, *let me in! let me in!*
Pull from my radiant
backpack the simple gravities

that keep me grounded:
my children's din
all nip and tuck before my feet,
or the astringent napkins
which I place daily on the supper table.

My graffiti grows and grows near
the cathedral's door, where the impulse
to enter is a black spider
whose gifts are few,
so I run, I run like the open field runner.

And at rest, though rest is always change,
I consider the death in men
and myself,
because the possibilities are endless.

Circle

Should we imagine death comes shining like a hero,
removes us from desire, and freed,
our pulsing electrons roam the universe?

Perhaps we settle in the catalpa tree,
gravitate to other ears in a bird's assonance,
or star-struck in the night, languish

a return to the physical, where drama and consequence
replay their karma to the critical masses.
No one stays if no one listens.

What is invisible constitutes the tangent
where air is gathered in a fist.
If everything's considered, nothing's left to chance.

Sundays, the church bells replay their echoes.
Children laugh, women dressed
in cardigan sweaters toss back their hair,

rejoicing in time like a Ming vase placed upon
the mantle. Our bodies soften,
our minds slow and crawl like spring

caterpillars in the catalpa tree.
We begin our journey to butterflies.
And the black birds pick us one by one.

Fear

I choose to recall it as perfunctory
the way the vascular surgeon considered me
through eyes dark as a mountain quarry,
yet deeper too, and unbroken—a piece of expensive porcelain

placed before me on the table, on which near commands
like sedentary lifestyle and amputation were laid out for me
to consider like appetizers for the palate. Indeed,
my swollen, phlebitis-filled leg, its pencil-thick
veins like nightcrawlers trying to surface

through the skin, seemed to be something
from a Stephen King novel, or a circus prop
that sometimes-brought shrieks from nieces and nephews
when I walked into a room. Twenty years ago, I was too young

to care much about what it meant to be afraid of anything.
But I could embrace fear in the way a bum embraces
a holeless pair of shoes. I feared I could not prove
the surgeon wrong; I feared the simplicity of giving up.

And so, I started to run and run until the leg turned purple
below the knee, and the veins boiled with pain:
first one mile, then two, then three or four at a time
until twenty years later, I'm still running with a friend

who many people believed would leave me.
Still some nights I dream back the surgeon's eyes,
a stainless saw in his hand, the operating room chatter,
above which I hear his monolithic voice explaining how
the beauty of nothingness can be replaced by prosthetic limb.

Notes from the Health Club

BMW's and SUV's dominate the parking lot,
as one old Bronco (mine) debases the asphalt.
Inside the front door, the nubile attendant greets
me with a forced smile, then continues
combing her platinum hair. Upstairs
on the treadmill, a court appointed attorney
labors a tortuous mile as his belly bounces
like a dune buggy over the desert.
Downstairs at the squat rack,
three metro narcotic detectives
with enormous thighs brag about last night's
big bust on Interstate Twenty. It seems
a carload of Mexicans crossed the center line.
Over at the lat machine is a Kiss-Me-Kate convention
of twenty-something sirens. Each has a runner's body,
a stewardess's smile, and the darkest tan
I've seen in March. They perform
minimal pulldowns with erotic discipline.
Testosterone snipers shuffle by them;
each centers his crosshair where
he imagines his bullets will fly.
And I wonder what they all think of me?
This quiet Vet with one damaged leg,
hair grown long, and three days unshaven,
is amicable as a weed. He is never found
near the incline press discussing politics,
the stock market, or high school sports.
Instead, he runs three miles at a rapid clip,
then not resting, moves on to crunches,
dips, pull-ups, benches three hundred pounds
for his final set. Nearing forty, he is now exhausted
but knows his workout is just starting.
He gathers his breath, sips some water,
walks outside into the night, pauses

briefly to consider the stars, their infinite
volume. Sweat continues down his face.
He smiles, then hurries home to write a poem.

The Mud Flats

My ten-year-old son trails behind me as I once trailed my father.
Both of them seem displaced, my father
now in his sixties, this tan boy his mother's pride.

He whistles, kicks up leaves, places twigs and stones
into his tiny backpack. I carry the .22 rifle
that I hope will shoulder him into manhood.

In the morning light we've been plinking cans,
watching the sun rise higher and higher,
as dark gray branches brighten into a greater green.

Beneath motionless clouds, we emerge from a strand
of oak and pine, deadfalls, and twisting vines,
at the mud flats where the marsh has receded under drought.

We stop as if tangled in thorns, stare out through the haze,
where thin as the reeds that surround it, a blue heron
struggles in the sucking mire. But it is the cat that calls us.

Its paws and face are muddy, it creeps slowly,
there is no separation between belly and earth.
I drop to one knee, eye the cat, center the crosshair

on its head. All I need do is pull the trigger. But I wait.
Like fingers on a piano's keys, my son's eyes dart
back and forth. The heron beats its paper wings,

cries out, fights to free its body to the sky.
The cat approaches until it is only yards away,
twitches along its length with one-thousands-years

of stalking instinct. How can I ever relive it—
the cat's coiled lunge to its certain prey,
heron, father, son, lifting into that pin-point moment

of ecstasy when the jumper clears the high bar.

This Morning

This morning, fallen perhaps from the great oak
beside the house, I found on the hood
of my green Suburban the body
of a white-throated sparrow.
For a moment, I believed it was not dead,
but a fist of feathers that would open and fly
back to settle in the branches above,
where other sparrows were singing death a song.

Minutes after a Louisiana sun cut
into the sky, the horizon showed orange creases.
A farmer's adage made me think a storm was coming.
Back east in Pennsylvania,
my father lay in his hospital bed,
a week removed from the surgery
that cut out his esophagus,
pulled up his stomach,
and attached it to his throat.

Cancer. It drives us from our wonderland,
and demands to know why
we have not been paying attention all along.
And even when the earth overflows with good things,
days like this rein them back.
After I brushed the sparrow to the ground,
I turned to find my black cat hunched in the kitchen window.
The way he looked at me!
It appeared as if he had not eaten in weeks…

As Fire, My Father

My father as fire melts December snow
with each step he takes through a Pennsylvania field.

But there is no field there is no snow,
only a mud-rutted road where my father walks

as fire under a sky filled with molten geese,
which now know the horror of too much heat.

My father as fire sits in a flat-bottomed boat.
He poles across the water, looking down into it,

where he sees a glowing town a city & pillows,
on which ashes shape themselves into children's faces,

& friends & former lovers & joyful leaps from remembered pets.
My father as fire believes in string theory & chaos,

convenience stores & muscle cars & the fly rod
abandoned to the cellar because fire & water no longer mix.

Some days the old rivers run through his eyes.
Some days his old eyes run through the rivers

like a diamond's facets like a snake's fangs,
like seven white horses drinking from a flaming trough.

My father as fire at seventy believes in the laying of hands,
an act which brings him both pleasure & pain,

the moment the father sees the son
close his eyes & begin to burn.

The Dying Cowboy

At night we came, wild men with horses.
Saddle-sore, cold, and in need of a drink.
Inside the dark saloon we passed the whiskey bottle
between us. Our throats burned
and with each drink we left the trail behind us.
Gone were cattle-drives, burnt coffee, and beans,
distances measured by buttes and deep ravines.
We were rawer than a scream,
rawer than any winter wind across the open range.
Our clothes were now too big,
our boots covered in the mud
we'd known for weeks. But the whiskey warmed us,
made us whole again, helped us forget
the smell from our unwashed bodies.
Carlos, bless him, had endured a broken tooth,
snapped flush at the gumline,
after biting down on some jerky.
And song? There was none. We could not sing.
We were still young and clumsy with things
we knew little about, garden flowers, parasols,
Sunday walks. Here he hesitated
and stared out of his hospital room window
at some Big Sky country.
My grandfather, the dying cowboy,
slipped a yellowed piece of paper into my hand.
He smiled as if he could bring back
the wind-driven cumuli throwing shadows
for hours across sandstone,
silt-green rivers where horses lowered their heads
to drink, their big-boned bodies silhouetted
against a blood-red sunset with all the spirits
these men knew and faced alone
in a country four million years old.
He didn't cry. Instead, he whispered

as if he believed someone might hear him:
a preacher, friend, or perhaps the lone wolf
whose proud easy gait made him feel more alive
than any man he ever knew. Our secret,
he said, while his eyes sped towards the universe,
which waited for him in the soundlessness
above the snowy mountains to the North.
Our secret, he repeated. She was my first love,
and I loved her more than your grandmother.
Is it a sin to have loved but then let love go?
I looked down at the paper and read what was written;
Don't let canyons come between Us.
Love, Amy, Montana, 1902.

Wrestling with God, Buddhism, and Quantum Physics

One fish swimming near the ocean's surface
sees sky and sun and moon as separate worlds.

Far off in a meadow trampled by whitetails feeding,
a wildflower loses its petals to the wind.

Miles later this wind stirs a widow to her window,
where she watches the pine-rocker rocking back and forth.

Her husband's dead memories return,
it leads to her having an out-of-body experience:

they are born again in the lighting's flash.
They watch dirt dancing in the molecules

and molecules dancing in the temporal
where emptiness could be the purest form of existence

in terms of the speculative stray cat, not Schrödinger's,
but the Buddha's whose suffering implicates its karma

with the infinite nature of its mind. Sometimes the light
illuminates our quantum life as the science of probability.

I am here. You are there. The big brick wall
that separates us might let us pass through if we try.

A single particle from any creature can exist
in several places at once. I see

my German Shepherd barking simultaneously
in London and Paris. I see the hooded monk

invoking a sibyl at evening vespers.
My Grandmother's rosary beads have gathered moss.

Our father who art, our father who art, art where?
Citizens of New Orleans East

would you tell me, will the trumpeter swan
ever return to nest in the Easy?

The End of Something

Summer, the last of it
In the garden, or

The grass scrubbed brown
From little rain, too much sun

The way it falls down
As rain might as blood might
Come to us

In dark earthy overtones, as when a vein
Might suddenly open, or
A man tries to run away

But does not make it.
Where did he think he could go?

My dog brings home an arm in his mouth
My cat a finger like a mouse.

Outside, I imagine gold teeth gleaning the sun,
Testicles hanging from eaves.

Apprentice
- For Hemingway

Before there was a clean, well-lighted place,
We knew rock-strewn dens with tiny fire rings,
And bits of flesh and parts of broken bones.
Upon our backs, we wore our hoary hides
To keep us warm enough to hunt again.
No soldier's home; we spent our nights in caves
Hearing the sounds ten thousand bats would make,
Where they huddled as one in the darkness.

Before there were book stores along the Seine,
Enough Absinthe to make an army tight,
And pounds of discourse, which we would carry
Around like silk-worms balanced in our palms,
We etched with rocks, drawing strange characters
Upon the walls. A very short story
Took shape in that place, the last good country
With its faithful bulls and summer people.

After the storm had passed, I found Paris
Where I learned that the light of the world
Often became the mother of a queen,
Or stodgy twins wrapped in the other's arms.
Some nights I tried to pray myself to sleep.
Some nights I dreamed about a sunken wreck,
One bleached body tangled in the gunnel,
The single storm it took to put him there.

Watcher
- For Wallace Stevens

A black bird sits in a bare tree,
or does the bare tree sit within the black bird,
or is winter repeating itself in the wind's turning
through a bare tree and a black bird?

Was it true that the black bird moved a bit,
or was it my index finger that moved
the wind that moved the branch a bit,
or did the wind, tree, and bird move as one?

The black bird flies from the bare tree,
or does the bare tree fall from the black bird,
or am I the casual glance from a stranger,
recalling one moment that never occurred?

Winter

One tree top where the crow sits in deepest winter
is not the same as where the winter sits
among the dark stones the river cannot bear away.

In glittering twilight, the village winters in frigid light,
far from the crow's cry and the tree top's temple.
There the air's alive with wood smoke,

a motion soft as it settles into winter sky.
And why does the crow's flight go unnoticed
against the cosmic dance, against the endless universe

where the little stars died out long, long ago?
Yet still their light winters on in frozen things
from long ago and in the winter streets

where people meet to talk of winter things.
And streams are frozen too, and the bright ice
winters well into the deepest night.

The mind of winter and of what winters well
need not hear the story the village tells.
Some days one can hear the snowman sing—

a first break of blue that was not there before,
as from a boy's eyes in deepest winter,
who sees the summer rise from frozen things.

Remembering Lycoming County

As delicate as the first light of day,
the requiem is complete
for your tree-lined,
moss-covered banks,
your towering spruce and pines,
unrecognizable in winters,
nights when the silence was as dark as a cave.
Everything is now swept away,
too far downstream to paddle back.
To return is to drown,
to feel your muscles ache and burn
when trying to surface anew
and suck in air
again, and again and again.

Northern Lights

Once I spent all day among a thicket of hemlock
and pine on the side of a hill heavy with mountain laurel
greening as the sun first arced its current through morning
trees until it became a single luminous ball high overhead
and the light seemed to shift and prism on the wide stream
below me bordered with rocks and wild grasses where
mayflies rising from the eddied water drew trout that
angled up from the bottom to kiss the surface with lips
a stranger to the soft loam of the forest floor and those
places in the high branches above me where the nesting
of unseen birds was something spiritual and I found myself
thinking that what if suddenly the world as I knew it no longer
existed and the tide of my breath stopped as quickly
as the sound of thunder passing at night where the voices
around me no longer cared and this rooty earth
had become a place to dream away the knotted body
and in waking saw my reflection in Northern Lights.

Hidden Pond

Reflected on the water's surface
was a second-growth loblolly pine.
I knelt to see the bark's uneven weave,

smell the odor of its summer pitch.
But too late, I did not see the coiled moccasin
with its angry tail beating the air,

or its diamond-shaped head preparing to strike
as lightning would the unassuming man.
The fangs were halfway home

to my outstretched hand,
when from some high and hidden place,
a squirrel dropped an acorn into the water.

I waited for the venom's searing burn
that would swell the arm into something
unbearable to any touch.

But there was only the ripple's undulating merge
from water to shore, its weightless travel.
There was no tree. No squirrel.

Nor any snake that could withstand that world.

Mount Kenya

One year of living in your foothills,
I am reclaimed by the earth,
reduced to fertile soil.

In Kikuyu language, you are called *Kirinyage,*
mountain of brightness.

In summer when the lower plains
filled with dust, I wandered the Nanyuki-Meru road
to Aberdares where I once watched
a single leopard staring at me
at twilight, eyes burning.
At night I heard hyenas crying,
imagined sadness descending from the sky.

You were always with me,
a fire that leaves no scar.

In Autumn before monsoons
assailed the hills, I returned
to my *mucii,* a hut topped with thatch,
my doorway facing *Kirinyage.*

Village elders told me,
if you love something immense
and beyond your reach, if your faith
is never diminished by famine or flood,
one night the stars will turn
into white talons and lift me to your summit.

I believe them.

Nest Building

Within the unnamed green bush in the back yard,
with its ugly tangle of branches, half-breed brambles

racing out, turning like wind, again and again came movement.
It was not a detail to imprint the eye, like a white sloop

adrift on a blue sea, or the red hue from fire at midnight.
No, its clarity was indecision, what the moth cannot feel

as it draws close to flame, something that sinks
when given weight, like this factory-stretched, pencil-tube

aluminum lawn chair, where moments before, wearing a headband
of sweat, I lay cloistered in Sunstone beneath May sun.

We are defined by what passes before us, perception,
the static in telephone lines, small sounds the ear entices

from the earth. But is illusion the necessity? In a few minutes
a robin emerges, it flies across the yard into a sprawl of oak trees,

and returns over and over, like the easy loop of a surgeon's stitch,
circling back to its origin. Cotton tufts, innumerable twigs, leaf-
pieces,

wind-dead grasses. These things are given flight, carried on invisible
trails, implanted with spun rhythms. Now, after two days the musical

drive nears completion. Nothing has changed that can be truly
measured,
or will change the world. But I have learned some things.

I want to spend my days to Zero, God-Great in my efforts,
sand-simple and humble in my existence.

Autumn Meditation at Stony Gap

Behind the ageless barn, cattle graze a grassy field.
Red-winged blackbirds ink the morning sky
above the old mill pond, muddy and high from recent rains.

Swamp willows circle its shore. As I come closer
to the water, swans lift into flight
as if they are preordained to displace the evening stars.

The wind approaches on its imaginary axis.
Fistfuls of leaves are flung from branches.
A blue jay in fine fettle screams at a squirrel.

A cardinal's red tongue plays a tiny piano.
I hear a given God within that song as a red wasp
hesitates into flight as if bound by invisible rope.

Twenty years after Nepal my rice bowl
continues to empty as I recall a Tibetan monk's words,
Men who make enemies, also make enemies of themselves.

I chant sixteen mantras to the sun on a farm
where the Jesus flower and Buddha weed grow as one.
Say that I am not like you, but a different man.

Someone who weeps for any creek that runs dry,
or a farmer who parades his plow like a medal.
What I know of life is no larger than a rat's nostril.

Tonight, among trees in the dark, close to the river's edge,
I'll listen for the footfalls of wild animals,
watch their yellow eyes, study their untamed freedom.

Nothing is brighter than what is learned in darkness.
Like a carpet of fire my life burns before me.

Reunion

Forty years after graduation,
we have returned to this old gymnasium,
its hardwood floor, the overhead tungsten lights
which shine on us with small town ambivalence.
When I was in high school, this place
seemed much larger, the crowd's roar
sounded to me like Madison Square Garden.
Today, I still hear that sweet naiveté calling,
but it's useless to try to distinguish it
as anything more than the sound of shifting sand.
Tables and chairs have been pulled from storage,
dusted, assembled in rows around which we
linger, laugh, eye composites of the former selves.
Still, the double chins, stately bellies,
and porcelain legs confirm that, indeed,
Elvis is dead. They make some reintroductions
necessary, an undesired protocol
in which the handshakes serve our diplomacy.
After a couple of quick whiskies, or a few beers,
our immediacies relax, we pinpoint our excesses:
the boats, the cars, the cost of suburbia on dead end streets.
We lie (not all of us) and tell each other
how we loved our jobs all of those years,
how it came together as it should have been.
Outside, it begins to rain with such intensity
the roof begins to show its leaks. Inside,
we practice our cliques as if forty years
have not passed. But it's always inevitable,
a few people are missing for various reasons.
Perhaps it's the delayed flight out of Memphis,
or the booze hound who could not wake up
this morning, or cancer's black bird,
which sits singing on an old friend's shoulder.
When the lights flicker three times in succession,

we move closer until we nearly touch.
This is what we have here, nothing elaborate,
only us, a hopeful microcosm of the world,
raising our drinks in admiration and respect,
making whole the deaths that we have known,
and working on these epitaphs not yet written.

After the Elegy
- For Carol Moran

A few footfalls among the elms.
Unnoticed by anyone, ants follow.

Two cumulus clouds linger
in an otherwise orderly blue sky—

Brunelleschi could not have made
his dome as perfect as this.

Last page, the burning book has burned.
Crows fly overhead. Their eyes are

tiny bits of tar in a timeless haze.
They go by where three horses are grazing.

No heaven. No hell. Only
the big rig moving down the interstate

past the empty porch swing, swinging.
Of dying young, nothing remains

but memories of what we give
to what has gone. Listen—

blade by blade the grass is singing.

www.ingramcontent.com/pod-product-compliance
Lightning Source LLC
Chambersburg PA
CBHW071355090426
42738CB00012B/3123